MW01229477

TYPHON DRU

Nicole Brossard

TYPHON DRU

Translated by Caroline Bergvall

REALITY STREET EDITIONS
1997

Published by
REALITY STREET EDITIONS
4 Howard Court, Peckham Rye, London SE15 3PH
and
6 Benhall Green, Saxmundham, Suffolk IP17 1HU

"Typhon dru" was previously published in French in
two editions by Collectif Génération: (1) limited to 20
similar but not identical copies, with illustrations by
Noël Dolla, 1989; (2) limited to 30 similar but not
identical copies, with photos, collages and sometimes
paintings by Christine Davis, 1990.
"La matière harmonieuse manoeuvre encore" was
previously published, with a different translation by Lise
Weil, in *The Massachussetts Review*, vol XXXI Nos 1 & 2,
spring/summer 1990.

Cover photograph by Wendy Mulford
Back cover photograph of Nicole Brossard by Germaine
Beaulieu
Typesetting by Ken Edwards

Printed & bound in Great Britain
by The Ipswich Book Company Ltd

A catalogue record for this book is available from the
British Library

ISBN: 1-874400-11-3

Funded by
THE
ARTS
COUNCIL
OF ENGLAND

A NOTE ON TRANSLATION

The difficulty and dilemma of translation lies of course in its tendency towards cultural appropriation. A "making French", to use Baudelaire's phrase in relation to his Poe translations, which would not only attempt to make the shift from the one language to the next imperceptible, but which would, more forcefully, seek to absorb "as French" the translated text. If writing is always about construction, translation is perhaps doubly so: not only a construction of writing but one which somehow calls up tensions in the translation language as it enters into dialogue with the original text. In the case of my translation of these two texts by Nicole Brossard, I have been interested in thinking about such tensions. Not how can I make this image or this word or this sentence in the French necessarily fit English turns and phrases and images best but rather how would the French (-Canadian) text strain English and what kind of textual play would this enable.

Nicole Brossard's project is one which has consistently explored and played with notions of cultural and poetic con-structedness. One which has sought, in particular, to strain our readings of the socialised, sexualised body through textual body. To allow the translation process to become a kind of building site for a "translated-English" seemed to me, in this sense, to provide an obvious methodological approach to her work. As such, I have tried to integrate, albeit in a subtle and punctual rather than generalised manner, to my writing-read-ing of Brossard's work, an additional layer of reading. A cross-lingual reading which would let the original text destabilise in places the language of arrival and bring about new connec-tions. Thus seeking to bring forward Brossard's texts while forcing up, not absorbing, the actuality of the translation: by allowing for some neologisms, split prepositions, inversions, syntactical links to indicate the double vision of this call and response. Voir double. Reconstructing her text as much as reflecting on the two languages.

Caroline Bergvall

La matière harmonieuse manoeuvre encore

Harmonious Matter Still Manoeuvres

je présume que le jour se lève à plusieurs
endroits et parce que cette pensée me vient au
milieu de la réalité et de ses poses
innommables, j'ai, pour témoigner du temps et
des langages mobiles, recours à cette pensée
que rien n'est trop lent, ni trop bref pour
l'univers

I presume day rises in different points and since this thought occurs to me in the midst of reality, its unnameable poses, I do, to bear witness of time languages mobile, take stock of the notion that nothing is too slow nor too brief for the universe

je sais que tout n'est pas dit parce que mon
corps s'est installé avec un certain bonheur
dans cette pensée et que parmi la secousse
inexplicable qui des mots fait trajet, eau vive et
tant la soif, je peux en liant les voyelles et le
dos des pensées me rapprocher, les yeux bridés
de fascination, de la mort et de son contraire

I know that all isn't said because my body
settles with a certain joy into such a thought
and somewhere in the inexplicable jolt presses
words on, water running as much thirst, I can,
by joining vowels and the hump of thoughts,
eyes slant fascinated, get closer to death and its
opposite

à cette heure tardive où la souplesse du regard
est à son comble et que la vie se tourne et
retourne entre le bleu et l'étonnante loi des
villes illuminées, à cette heure tardive où les
mots se tiennent la poitrine comme dans les
opéras et que les images guettent le tracé lièvre
de la fièvre et du futur, mes yeux bien bas
penchés sur l'humanité s'inquiètent à partir de
la racine des yeux du désir

at this late hour where a suppleness of gaze is at its height and life turns returns between the blue and the startling law of high-lighted cities, at this late hour where words clasp their chest as in operas, and images look out for the jumpy tracks of fever and the future, my eyes lowered low over humanity are troubled at the root of eyes desire

tout n'est pas dit car je le sais, c'est absolument
que j'aime dans les langues, les coquilles roses
de sens, les structures assidues qui greffent
extases et chose torrentielle au milieu de la
voix et de son comportement, matière secrète,
matière plus ronde, matière comme tes soupirs
et d'autres liquides encore

all isn't said, I do know, since it's absolutely
that I love in tongues, coral shells of meaning,
the diligent structures that graft rapture and
torrential stuff on to the centre of the voice its
stance, secret matter, matter more round,
matter like your sighs and other liquids yet

aujourd'hui je sais que la structure la plus bleue
de la mer se rapproche de nos cellules et de la
souffrance intouchable comme la vie fait trois
fois le tour de notre enfance sans jamais y
toucher vraiment parce qu'on est proche de la
réalité et que la matière ne peut pas tomber
sans nous avertir, nous laisser là, la peau
hésitante entre les philosophies et l'aube, à
moitié, à jamais dans le tourment, dans la vaste
complication de la beauté

today I know that the most blue sea-structure
closes in on our cells and on the suffering
untouchable just as life does three times a
round our childhood never really touches on it
since we're close up to reality and matter can't
let down without a warning strand us there
skin hesitating between philosophies and
dawn, too halved, forever in torment, in the
major complication of beauty

tout n'est pas dit puisque le corps est
ponctuel et qu'il reste, versions de passion,
des gestes rares, une incroyable synchronie
des sens alors que la pensée, toujours en bonne
position d'alliance, veille à refaire dans la
tête le décor et d'anciens portraits imaginés
symétriques à notre enfance;
car il y a des traits qui nous reposent
pendant que nous creusons l'univers avec nos
épaules et de toutes petites lèvres imaginées
qui travailleraient sans merci dans le souci
de la vie à nous inventer le monde et le cosmos
à la mesure de nos mains quand elles
caressent bien, indistinctement de la voix et
de la paume, le corps humain qui a des seins

all isn't said since the body's punctual and there remains, read: passion, rare gestures, an incredible synchrony of the senses, while thought, such well-placed alliance ensures a retake in the mind, the setting the old portraits, their imagined symmetry with childhood, lines that give us rest while we burrow the universe with our shoulders, and tiny fantasised lips would be working ceaselessly for the living making up world and cosmos to the measure of our hands whenever their caress is fine, indistinct of voice and palm, on a human body has breasts

à cette heure tardive je sais que la vie peut
confirmer le silence, incendier les approbations,
tracer des larmes circulaires et la poussière
enfanter; et j'aime qu'il en soit ainsi car j'ai
appris à regarder, entre juillet et octobre, tous
les incendies, à m'imbiber de la forte odeur de
la nudité de la splendeur des mauves, des
façades et des sonnets étranges qui gesticulent
dans la langue comme nous le faisons la nuit en
rêvant pour ne pas mourir sans voix

at this late hour I know that life can confirm
silence set fire to commendations trace up
circular tears breed dust, and I like that it's so
since I've learnt to watch July to October all
fires, immerse myself in the strong smell of
nakedness its splendour mauves, the facades
and peculiar sonnets that gesture across
language like we do dreaming at night not to
die without voice

tout n'est pas dit et voilà que je m'élance avec
ma peau chargée de cyprine et d'écho parce
que j'ai envie de sourire, physique et pensante,
inséparable d'une nature au souffle long; ainsi
quand je regarde des objets stables et que dans
ma poitrine le temps s'inverse, fend la pensée,
d'un bond élucide la mort, je sais que tout
n'est pas dit parce que j'ai le coeur serré

all isn't said it's here I dash towards, my skin full of cyprin of echo feel like smiling physical and thinking, inseparable from a nature's long breath, so when I watch stable objects when time reverses in my chest splits the thought with a jump clarifies death I know that all isn't said because my heart's rucked up

à cette heure tardive où la mémoire a peur de
ses bonds et que les nerfs au milieu du désir
sont comblés de réponses, je sais que tout n'est
pas dit, je sais que la lumière quand elle
fracture l'ombre ranime en moi le respect de
l'ombre et de la lumière, je sais que débordant
dans l'air d'énergie, la vie qui est mienne
m'engage loin à souffler de près dans ma main
les images longues de la nécessité et, du
sentiment les belles brèches sur fond de rêve et
d'identité

at this late hour where memory's wary of its
jumps and nerves in the midst of desire are
rich with answers I know that all isn't said I
know when light fractures shadow revives my
consideration of shadow and light I know that,
brimming air energy, the living which is mine
takes me far to breathe closer to hand the long
images of necessity and of sentiment are
gorgeous cracks against a backdrop of
dreaming and identity

à cette heure tardive où nommer est encore
fonction de rêve et d'espoir, où la poésie
sépare l'aube et les grands jets du jour, et que
plusieurs fois des femmes s'en iront invisibles et
charnelles dans les récits, je sais que tout n'est
pas dit parce que, entre la conversation urbaine
et la tradition, il fait froid dans le vertige et que
parfois dans la matière volatile des larmes une
étrange sueur de vrai s'installe comme si la vie
pouvait toucher ses métaphores

at this late hour where to name is still a
function of the dream of the hope, where
poetry splits daybreak from great gushes of
daylight, and women will walk a number of
times, invisible carnal into the storylines, I
know that all isn't said, between urban
conversation and tradition it's cold in vertigo,
and sometimes in the volatile matter of tears a
peculiar sweat of true settles as if life could
touch its metaphors

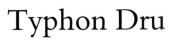

Typhon Dru

et c'est l'envol vagues typhon dru
comme un coude dans la nuit
rai de mœurs
le monde est vite obscur

partout où la bouche est excentrique
il neige et quelque chose est chaud
sous la langue, le moi s'enroule émoi
plane ruban de joie
paupières harmoniques

and this is lift-off breakers typhondru
like an elbow in the night
slit of ways
the world drops quickly

every where mouth is eccentric
it snows something's warm
under tongue the self coils anticipation
glides joy ribbon
eyelid harmonics

car le monde est vite obscur
et la nuit me rend avide
de partout frôle tant
que la langue avec son sel
un à un les verbes les troue
de silence, typhon dru

because the world drops
quickly and night makes me crave
through and through brushes so
that the tongue its salt
one by one riddles
verbs with silence, typhondru

en plein vol si j'ouvre les bras
mes cheveux sont lents dans l'oxygène
je prétends qu'il y a de vastes lois
au-delà des villes et des sépultures
ruban de voix, lame des yeux

ce soir si tu rapproches ton visage
et que la civilisation s'étire
au bout de tes bras, ce soir
si en plein vol tu rattrapes mon image
dis que c'était au loin
comme un dé dans la nuit

in full flight if I open my arms
my hair is slow with oxygen
I pretend there are vast laws
beyond cities and sepulchres
voice ribbon, eye current

tonight if you bring your face in
and civilisation stretches
out to your arms end tonight
if in full flight you pull my image up
say in the distance there was
like a dice in the night

et pendant que mon sexe songe à l'aurore
mouille muqueuses heureuses
il neige et la proximité encore
je prétends que c'est l'aura
ou l'image asymétrique
de l'image brève en plein vol

and while my sex thinks of daybreak
soaks mucously beaming
it snows and proximity still
I pretend it's the aura
or the asymetric image
of a briefly imaged in full flight

lame de fond, cérémonie de l'image
mon cœur est agile
l'émotion entre nous
matière du rire, matière c'est vrai
et ma voix qui craque
dans le froid rose des galaxies

undercurrent, ceremony of the imaged
my heart is agile
this emotion between us
materialises laughter, material indeed
and my voice snaps
in the galaxies' cold coral

je prétends veiller en silence
dans le froid rose des galaxies
je prétends que si l'œil est noir
il ne peut pas veiller

partout où la bouche rieuse virtuelle
d'énergie dévore l'aube déverse son oui
elle crie du mieux qu'elle jouit
tympan, mauves sonores
vastes lois qui lèchent
au loin le fond de l'air

I pretend to be watching in silence
in the galaxies' cold coral
I pretend that if the eye is dark
it cannot keep watch

every where a teasing mouth of virtual ener
gy devours dawn discharges yes
cries out for better she comes
eardrum resonant mauves
vast laws that lick
a far the air drum

au matin *e* plane haut
et les rivières sont longues
sous ma peau d'autant de parcours
à saveur de femme et de lucidité
au matin, la rivière est haute
quand je te touche
face à face dans l'affirmation

by morning her glides high
and rivers are long
under my skin they're many routes
cream of woman and of lucidity
by morning the river's high
when I touch you face
to face in affirmation

NICOLE BROSSARD

Nicole Brossard was born in Montreal in 1943. Poet, novelist and essayist, she has published more than 20 books since 1965. Among these: *A book, Daydream Mechanic, Picture Theory, French kiss, The Aerial letter* and *Mauve Desert*. By her ludic, subversive and innovative work on language, Brossard has influenced a whole generation on the questions of post-modernist and feminist writing. She also co-founded the important literary periodicals *La Barre du Jour* (1965) and *La Nouvelle Barre du Jour* (1977). In 1976, she co-directed the film *Some American Feminists*. Ms Brossard was twice awarded Canada's most prestigious prize, the Governor General's Award for poetry, in 1974 and in 1984. She was also given Le Grand Prix de Poésie 1989 de la Fondation Les Forges and in 1991 she was awarded Le Prix Athanase-David (the highest literary recognition in Quebec literature). *Mauve Desert* has been translated into English, Spanish, German and Dutch. The American critic Karen Gould has written about her work: "The contributions of Nicole Brossard to contemporary literature and literary theory and their inevitable intersection through feminist thought have been visionary."

CAROLINE BERGVALL

Caroline Bergvall is a poet and a performance writer. She has developed performances and installations with other artists and was awarded the Showroom Live Art Commission 1993 for her choral poem *Strange Passage* (Equipage, 1993). Recently she published *Éclat* (Sound & Language, 1996) and her work is in the anthologies *Out of Everywhere* (Reality Street Editions, 1996) and *Conductors of Chaos* (Picador, 1996).

Other titles published by Reality Street Editions:

Cris Cheek/Sianed Jones: *Songs From Navigation*
Kelvin Corcoran: *Lyric Lyric*
Allen Fisher: *Dispossession and Cure*
Susan Gevirtz: *Taken Place*
Fanny Howe: *O'Clock*
Sarah Kirsch: *T*
Maggie O'Sullivan: *In the House of the Shaman*
Denise Riley: *Mop Mop Georgette*
Peter Riley: *Distant Points*

Out of Everywhere: linguistically innovative poetry by women in North America & the UK (ed. by Maggie O'Sullivan)

RSE 4Packs No. 1: *Sleight of Foot* (Miles Champion, Helen Kidd, Harriet Tarlo, Scott Thurston)